Made in the USA
Middletown, DE
07 August 2023

36268513R00120